Note About The Author

Austin Kaiser is a writer from South Amboy, New Jersey. He writes about art and imagination and plans to publish a series of books on the subjects. He'll publish not only himself but other authors interested in creative processes and art studies. If you'd like to read his work or submit your own, visit @AdviceForArtists on Instagram. *Someday, there will be a renaissance.*

Feel Free To Feel Free

Secrets Of The Universe

Condensed Into Clever

One-Liners

By Austin Kaiser

Dedicated

to forever young students,

with love,

to Malory for illustrating this incredible cover,

to Ciara for voicing the audio version,

to my gaggle of friends who have lent me beds, dollars, and company,

to my family who lent me genes, role models, and meals,

and to you who lent me your time.

Contents

1. Life is a parade of circuses.

2. Fun fathers freshness.

3. Set aside time so you can lose track of it.

4. If you study enough, one day you will be studied.

5. There is a temple between your temples.

6. A skill is a skill when you can do it at will.

7. Choose your profession based on which will give you the most orgasms.

8. It is only a matter of time before this moment becomes nostalgic.

9. Walking is meditation with a view.

10. Studying history helps you realize that it just started.

11. Life teaches you how to live it if you live long enough to learn it.

12. It takes practice to say, 'I love you.'

13. To think is to fish your mind's sea.

14. How to solve a problem: 1) breathe 2) allow time to elapse.

15. Dumb luck has a plan for you.

16. Take breaks — that's when you get a lot of work done.

17. A museum is what you get when a genius is a hoarder.

18. Ride the elephant in the room.

19. Obvious genius is hidden everywhere.

20. Studying irrelevant art proves there is no such thing.

21. Life is a love-led lottery.

22. If you are scared, it means you are close to a new source of courage.

23. 'Glass half full' is more accurate.

24. Swimming in the ocean is like living in a painting.

25. Why there have been problems since The Beatles released the song 'All You Need Is Love' is a mystery.

26. After accomplishing something difficult, the next trick is making it look effortless.

27. I am a slacker who works everyday.

28. It takes a couple of years to become a beginner.

29. It takes a couple more to become a natural.

30. Intuition is when your first guess is the right guess.

31. Truth is to art what water is to rain because when you drop truth on someone's head, it turns into art.

32. Reading a good sentence is like having a gun go off by your ears.

33. Danger is a good opportunity to practice being nonchalant.

34. As you gain advantages, it becomes easier to gain advantages.

35. Sometimes sandcastles wash on shore.

36. Life goes from a box of crayons to a box of wine to a box of pine.

37. Tulip or not to leap, that is the question.

38. You can take a man to Google but you can't make him search.

39. The only difference between thinking and writing is whether or not your chair is reclined.

40. You're an idiot if you don't think you're a genius.

41. I don't have a writing style as much as I have a ranting style.

42. Change is ever-present, innovation is ceaseless, and the thing you make that will startle the world will be a product of your freedom, spontaneity, intuition, and unembarrassed heart.

43. When your dues are paid and you have experienced the art-making process enough to consider yourself a resident of it like a gardener does their garden or a surfer does their wave, you reach bliss, the post-fluctuation, steady pleasure, also known as grace, flow, oneness, connectedness, all-encompassing mind, body, spirit, past, present, future 'yes'-ness.

44. For proper creativity, it helps to have both Mary Shelley's fiction and Marie Curie's fact.

45. Your inventions invent inventions.

46. Good actors aren't acting.

47. Every song is its own genre.

48. In the space between your pen and paper, a world fidgets.

49. Making art is like driving with no other cars on the road.

50. Sometimes the most productive thing you can do is stare out the window.

51. If you are alive, you are young.

52. Collect things that collect dust.

53. The simplest person on Earth is enormously complex.

54. I have yet to find an obstacle that can withstand persistence.

55. To learn a fact is to add a suspension cable to the bridge that connects you to the truth.

56. The only difference between you and a photographer is that the photographer decided to take a picture.

57. Take a risk to practice taking risks.

58. Writing is a promise to your past self, 'I did not forget you.'

59. Life is running from birthday to birthday and seeing how many presents you can unwrap.

60. A genius is someone who knows how to love.

61. Anytime there is no renaissance, everyone is waiting and ready for a renaissance.

62. Trying is the most reliable way of getting better.

63. Feel free to feel free.

64. Life happens live.

65. Waking up is a good way to start the day.

66. Life is a date you go on with yourself.

67. You are the only person with your perspective. So, as a moral businessperson with a monopoly over a natural resource would do, you, who has a natural monopoly over your ideas, must share them.

68. To all doors, effort is entry.

69. Axioms produce offspring.

70. The fact that all kids from all countries and religions enjoy toilet humor is proof that some shit is just funny.

71. Learn to write so you get your money's worth from the Freedom of Speech.

72. Freedom of Speech means everybody gets to write their own Declaration of Independence and Constitution.

73. Freedom of Speech is how you know you're free; if you have it, you are and if you don't, you aren't.

74. Civilization without freedom of speech is just lip syncing.

75. Freedom of Speech is the only philosophical idea that came screaming into the world.

76. Anyone can write powerfully because sincerity is powerful and anyone can be sincere.

77. I would not wish pessimism on my worst enemy.

78. Time and good vibes heal all wounds.

79. Realistically, you should fall in love all the time.

80. The one thing an artists must do if they hope to become great is poop their pants in public. (It means they are completely comfortable

expressing their innermost self in any circumstances. (Warning: this is a metaphor))

81. Anything the brain does multiple times, it learns.

82. We could all just be part of a really long Shakespeare monologue.

83. Genius is re-invented every time someone is born.

84. Ideas are flammable.

85. You can be good at anything in six months. Everything after that is the infinite road to mastery.

86. Go to the movies and close your eyes and listen to the writing.

87. When you turn to writing, you return.

88. Pursue happiness persistently.

89. Use the skills learned during the small victories to win the big victories.

90. Your work better be ahead of its time because the present just happened a minute ago.

91. Use the pen like a scapegoat — blame it on the pen.

92. Sing something unsung.

93. The bigger the meteor, the bigger the crater.

94. Art is the horse and we are the carriage.

95. Many breakthroughs come from someone just trying.

96. When I open up to you, I open up to myself.

97. You can give and receive all of life's information if you are open-minded and talkative.

98. Beginnings are always beginning.

99. To be a better artist, be a better person.

100. History is divided into eras and 'isms for convenience but the actual content of history are individuals.

101. The media doesn't like the way the media is portrayed in the media.

102. The first try is clumsy and the hundredth is smooth.

103. Amnesia the mistakes and deja vu the success.

104. Our prehistoric ancestors wondered, "What would it be like to be free? Who would we become if given a chance to be ourselves for a lifetime? What if the passion that went into de-fanging a saber-toothed tiger was put towards philosophy, academia, theater, painting, partying, friendship, and movie nights?"

105. Athleticism requires creativity and creativity requires athleticism.

106. One of the best parts of being awake is going to sleep.

107. The road to flow goes: make art, release art, learn from the impact, repeat.

108. Practice is doing something on purpose right now so you can do it automatically later.

109. You are lying on an island as big as your silhouette.

110. Ever since the internet and airplanes, the world became one destination where information flows.

111. A first draft should be an act of love and being impulsive is the quickest way to fall in love.

112. The imagination can contemplate ideas so distant that they are in the future.

113. Art is yoga for the imagination.

114. The two times you get to know people best are during crises and when you two are sitting on a couch, doing nothing.

115. The time between the moment you realize you need to change your behavior and the moment it changes is the time it takes to break and replace a habit.

116. Knowledge begins as guessing about generals and becomes guessing about specifics.

117. People are engineers, doctors, plumbers, chauffeurs, and parents of ideas.

118. Conversations are idea movers.

119. Swivel your eyes like satellite dishes.

120. I can show you only as much as can fit in a keyhole.

121. Sometimes my humble side has trouble submerging the feeling, 'I am really good at what I do.'

122. Second nature is what happens when effort becomes effortless.

123. On the importance of whim: by indulging in creative work for no reason, you ready yourself to do creative work for some reason.

124. I write as a profession and a hobby which means that if I have free time, I'm writing and if I'm busy, I'm writing.

125. Art is the water and you are the waterfall, the fish, and the lifeguard.

126. I'm young for my age.

127. A great joy of being a critic is knowingly subjecting yourself to the effects of art.

128. An urge is when you want something even though you're not trying to want it.

129. Bob Dylan opened for Dr. Martin Luther King's "I Have A Dream" speech.

130. To be light-hearted means to, at an unconscious level, know that everything will be alright and why everything will be alright and, at a conscious level, crack a joke about the situation.

131. Confidence is a sun you can summon.

132. An artist should be three things: curious, hungry for knowledge, and interested in learning.

133. Be nosy for knowledge, insatiable for insight, and curious for queries. That'll ensure a mind that can meddle in mental magic, most definitely. How nice it is to whisk whim like whirligigs and coif concepts like carnival cotton candy. These are the delights of a developed dome piece, the pleasures of a primed pituitary. Please, do pass time with powerfully dreamt ponderences. Those are the rewards and rights of passage that all reasonably reigned and honestly honed hubris hopefully have.

134. The world has an appetite for worlds.

135. A good editor can look at a turd and say, "I see the good here."

136. Diplomas and dollars are optional papers.

137. The brain is omnivorous.

138. This stuff, added to yesterday's stuff, becomes cumulative stuff.

139. Your job is to perceive the world and write down your reaction.

140. I am proud of you for being proud of yourself.

141. I love peace — are you into peace?

142. When it gets windy, wait under the mango tree.

143. A snob is someone who used to learn for love but now learns to feel superior.

144. If you want your writing to be timeless, write for the re-reader.

145. Good words = sugar; good ideas = medicine

146. You have too much courage to be discouraged.

147. Artists are interior decorators (by interior, I mean, the interior of one's head).

148. Create things that redden cheeks, water eyes, and clench fists.

149. Sometimes it's appropriate to incubate. Other times, it's time to hatch. The questions is, how fidgety is your beak?

150. Going viral is the shortest distance between an idea in an inventor's mind and an idea in everyone's mouth.

151. Admiring art is admiring the variety and depth of impressions the mind can feel.

152. Perfectionism is that thing that seems like it helps but doesn't.

153. Greedily seek the next milestone.

154. Squeeze action and oxygen into art and make a cultural ka-boom.

155. My art is good today, progresses tomorrow, and the pattern repeats itself infinitely.

156. Your brain is a Large Hadron Collider.

157. Some ideas have fifteen mommies and daddies.

158. It's all waiting behind a door labeled, 'Time.'

159. My cat lays in all places as if it's laying in a hammock.

160. The first one to succeed is the last one to pant.

161. Do whatever you want with your life as long as you keep making art.

162. At some point in the future, I am going to come up to you and say, 'Didn't I tell you this was going to happen?'

163. Anyone can happen.

164. Dare faster.

165. Heal aggressively.

166. Life is very very very very very very very fresh.

167. The subconscious is like a mailman that reads your mail and occasionally writes in it.

168. Open your face and fall out.

169. When I write a good sentence, I feel like a proud caveman standing over his fire screaming, "FIREEEEEEEEEEEEEE.

170. A kiss is an artistic medium.

171. Practice makes hard things easy.

172. Whisper loudly.

173. Museums should give out folding chairs at the door.

174. I want art to be taken seriously so it is no longer serious.

175. Think of how big your lungs would be from the sighs of relief that come after being told to smash all watches, unplug all clocks, and sink all electronic time keepers.

176. Every person has a library in their mind and the more books you read, the more books are on the shelves.

177. I'm in love with artists but I'm not yet in love with how they're educated.

178. Artists should indulge in Totoro and Tarantino and Breakfast at Tiffany's and Pixar's Toy Story and Chan's Police Story trilogies.

179. We need Keith Haring collaborating on a comic strip with Charlie Brown and Charles Shultz.

180. Some artists think about art in the shower and before they fall asleep and they find the desire to make art sneak up out of nowhere, for no reason.

181. It's hard to kill a giant so celebrate every inch of the beanstalk you chop.

182. A white canvas makes the wild west look like a flea market.

183. Learn how to love your loves.

184. A poet is a person who places pieces of paradise between periods.

185. If a thoughtful person shares their thoughts, I am a thoughtful listener.

186. Tell it like it is, like, "That's how it is."

187. If you tell the truth, people will understand what you're saying.

188. Practice is the essence of finesse.

189. Almost any behavior can be excused if it looks like someone is doing it for the right reasons.

190. Being on a roll means getting carried away.

191. Some ideas are like zombies, coming out from old ideas you thought were dead.

192. Being an artist includes being a librarian of your mind.

193. One of the world's most compelling things is a person's face experiencing emotion.

194. Either in the stock market or in a relationship, you may need to let go of a loser even though you don't want to.

195. We become emotional when someone clashes or conforms with our beliefs.

196. Empathy is someone else's feelings happening inside you.

197. Learning how to communicate means learning how to communicate with your art, others, and yourself.

198. As the average communications skills of people rise, so does their peace and cooperation.

199. Art is like taking your feeling and packing it into a snowball.

200. Art is like taking your feeling and packing it into a shot glass, cherry seed, candle wick, grass blade, fish hook, prosciutto slice, bird's nest.

201. Art is the best part of being a person.

202. Art is in everyone's top 3 best parts of being a person.

203. Top 2

204. Top 1

205. Art is anything that leaves an impression.

206. Art is expressing yourself and feeling other people's expressions.

207. Art is when you take a pizza knife and cut a strip of life and stretch it over a canvas so people can see what it's really like.

208. Art is throwing a football with a whistle.

209. Art is the feeling of growing another tree ring in you.

210. Art is putting the address you mean to send a letter to in the place for the sender's address so that when you mail it without a stamp, the post office returns it to the person you wanted it to get to.

211. Art is holding a piece of yourself up to the sun.

212. You are the Michael Jordan of being yourself.

213. Sometimes it's smart to rely on dumb luck.

214. The more talented you get, the more your realistic expectations grow to the size of your idealistic expectations.

215. You're just a person with a little bit of unlimited talent.

216. We are alive for our entire lives.

217. At some point in being an art fan, you become an archaeologist.

218. We know accurately what we relearn.

219. Love is the son of fun.

220. Every song should have a Stairway To Heaven version.

221. An open-minded mind gets fed.

222. If it speaks to you, speak to it.

223. Friends are people who know your loudest laugh.

224. I really enjoy watching a young writer write and fortunately I get to see that everyday.

225. I'm happy when I cry.

226. Sometimes you discover the meaning of life when you're too drunk to remember it.

227. If I lived forever, I'd read every scrap of paper that Shakespeare ever sneezed on.

228. Lifetime tickets to every museum as well as summer passes to every beach is a constitutional right.

229. Somewhere inside your pink meatloaf, is a space that always has more room, a room that always has more space.

230. Just because I'm having trouble with it doesn't mean it's not easy.

231. There are some things that you cannot see unless you light all of the candles.

232. Run on the treadmill until it explodes.

233. If you want to discover alien life, put a telephone on the moon.

234. I was looking for the other m&m I brought with me and I realized it was in my other cheek.

235. Check that garbage bag because one out of a million might be full of money.

236. Run towards the explosion. While everyone else is running away, you'll get there, see something unique, and be able to turn it into art.

237. Carmelo Anthony on the origins of Hoodie Melo, "Actually it started with a beanie."

238. Scent sells.

239. Every work of art made is another log on the fire of your life.

240. There is no difference between improving as an artist and being awake.

241. I have a habit of being a creature of habit.

242. Not being ambidextrous is expensive.

243. You can go to town exponentially longer if you can hold your breath for more than two minutes which isn't too hard to do if you practice consistently.

244. You don't have to like a song to like it.

245. Whatever happened to the present moment that I was supposed to live in?

246. Everybody has a voice to voice.

247. Animate a fossil.

248. Sometimes you have to catch yourself in a trust-fall.

249. Being the change you want to see in the world is a hell of a lot of work.

250. Life is a long tongue twister.

251. How much can you love if you get past its issues?

252. The angel on my shoulder has a devil on its shoulder and the devil on my shoulder has an angel on its.

253. Always go outside on a sunny, winter afternoon.

254. The only time I was wrong was the time I thought I was wrong.

255. I misplaced the ticket for my train of thought.

256. As soon as I discover what I'll invent, then I'll know.

257. 'I can't recommend it too highly' is a compliment or an insult depending on whether you say use 'to' or 'too.'

258. Pray to Miyazaki.

259. Childhood is not a long enough time to explore childhood.

260. It's awesome when you like something instantly and it still grows on you.

261. Sometimes life is like a musical and you do just start singing for no reason.

262. You need your imagination to commit empathy.

263. You can't trip when you're kicking it.

264. There is a lot of sea to see.

265. Sometimes short-term memory

266. Rap is the world's most popular literature.

267. Whenever my imagination writes something outrageous and catches me off guard, I think, "Yep, there it is again: anything."

268. Fashion is personality plus clothing.

269. Writing is personality plus words.

270. Every day begins with a fade in and ends with a fade out.

271. Anybody can relate with anybody if they want to.

272. My life is on the other side of the shuffle button.

273. If it ain't made with love, I'll have a slice to be polite.

274. Truth has children.

275. I was born kissing.

276. Life is long enough to do anything but too short to do everything.

277. How to succeed: 1) Be born 2) Make art.

278. Art works in mysterious ways.

279. I raise my hand first and think of what to say second.

280. When you fish for fish sometimes a thought is caught.

281. To become a good writer, write a million word as quickly as you can.

282. Enjoy joy.

283. Flex a brain muscle, squirt an imagination turd.

284. A beautiful thing about a relationship is having someone else be committed to being your second brain.

285. Planned spontaneity is knowing beforehand that you will lose control.

286. Work on art because art works on you.

287. Earth is a blink and the afterlife is a gaze.

288. To learn from libraries is to have the torch passed to you and to drive by the library without ever going in it to have the torch passed over your head.

289. Each person is a universe.

290. Destiny is as real as you think it is.

291. Light-heartedness is the shock absorber of life.

292. You have a beach between your ears.

293. Prolific artists are good enough for a sushi menu's variety to appear on their canvas on a slow day.

294. Every generation is in the mood to think.

295. The best part of trying is the habit it trains.

296. A prolific writer can write a novel in a straight jacket.

297. A younger sister is someone to look up to.

298. When an art writer whose job it is to translate art to words needs a writer to translate their words to common language then they have given a brick when they could have given a home.

299. How to be better: 1) practice 2) allow time to elapse.

300. Knowing what your favorite things in the world are means knowing where to aim your rocket.

301. An artist is a sandcastle builder on the beach of the imagination of the audience.

302. Having something to say is what keeps an artist prolific.

303. One person can try 3.2 million styles.

304. When you think of the experience a brain has when it reads a book and you put that side-by-side with the experience it has when it watches a film, and again with the experience it has when it's living off the land with access to no books or movies, you think, "What diversity, what infinite shapes this pink wad can take on, and what impressions can be left on it, and what wonders it can then perform with those impressions…."

305. Art studies is the study of all that art has done for us and can do and yet the study is rarely studied and only is it studied when we want something done at which point the things previously done which we could be studying from have not yet been turned into study material.

306. Be sensitive to your sensations.

307. Concentrate on your concentrations.

308. Knowing that you can always try again is like knowing the gumball machine always returns the quarter.

309. Vision is what you see with your eyes open. Artistic vision is what you see with them closed.

310. Lil Wayne is a painter.

311. Optimism is optimal.

312. A paint brush is a spear.

313. Every work of art is a universe.

314. Be knowledgeable about your knowledge and don't be ignorant of your ignorance.

315. How to change an attitude from fear to relaxation: make sense of it then make light of it.

316. Your art bites the tail of your life and your life returns the favor.

317. Even trash is cash.

318. An interviewer's job is to bring the culture out of a person.

319.	Libraries are where intellectuals have orgies. There you'll find people's gaping minds being penetrated by naked truths.

320.	An old wise man once told me that great artists are able to poop their pants in public. I said, "Jeez. What does that mean?" The old wise man said, "They are able to be completely comfortable expressing something strange, knowing that those around them find it strange too." I said, "That makes some sense but it's an awfully weird metaphor." He said, "I know. The advice itself illustrates my point perfectly though. It's a strange idea and I felt comfortable telling you." Then he got up and ran to the bathroom. He was truly a wise old man. (This is #80's poop metaphor in story form.)

321.	If no one is talking about the elephant in the room then you should jump on that elephant and ride it around and, while you're at it, whip out your magic Dumbo feather and get it flying. Suddenly, everybody who was playing dumb a second ago will wipe elephant footprints from their foreheads and say, "Oh, that elephant. That's what you were talking about." You fly away happy, knowing that you told the truth and did so in style.

322.	A good actor can convince the grim reaper that they've got the wrong guy.

323. One of the most important things to an artist is their intellectual and creative trajectory, also known as the growth of their mind, and it's something that only they can really understand because they are the ones who lived it. This is why, even if job opportunities are sparse and external achievements are lacking, the artists themselves can know with certainty that they are doing well and, in fact, are doing extraordinary. Their personal development is their satisfaction source.

324. The *it* factor is someone thriving as themself. Their self expression is free and everyday, a natural outgrowth of an active personality.

325. If you can walk, you can dance. If you can talk, you can write. If you can breathe, you can write.

326. Art we do everyday: dressing, cooking, joking, shower singing, and self-loving. Face painting, diary writing, and home movie filmmaking if schedule allows.

327. Sometimes any thinking is overthinking. If your intuition naturally comes up with the right answer, let it be.

328. If you want your audience to respond to your work, create something that can be agreed or disagreed with. This is going to either disturb or reinforce a belief of theirs and they'll respond accordingly.

329. For adrenaline junkies, read the speeches of Martin Luther King Jr. out loud. Feel what it would have been like to be Martin, to stand at a podium and share those thoughts with people whose minds had lived in a world that had perfectly prepared them to hear the words. There is driving a fast car, visiting a casino, asking someone attractive for their number — there are a lot of ways to get a rush and reading these speeches aloud is one of them.

330. Confidence is my chaperone.

331. Homework: read one poem per day, one essay per day, one movie per week, one book per month.

332. 7 Times In The Shower: you time, think time, sing time, wash time, routine time, prepare time, and self-love time.

333. Do you ever just wake up on a Sunday and feel like a blank slate and act like it's your first day on Earth? These days are fun and leave a great afterglow.

334. The all-time heavyweight undefeated most important thing for an artist is flow. Flow, flow, flow. Flow is home. Flow is the answer. When a flow flows through you, you flow into the flow of art history. Flow is that feeling of forgetting there is such a thing as 'art' or 'flow' and instead doing — happily, focusedly, naturally doing. For ten minutes,

or maybe ten hours per day, flow is the daily ritual that leads to success skills-wise, finance-wise, and personal fulfillment-wise.

335. The thing about breaking personal boundaries is that some you don't realize are there until you break them. You find yourself in a new state of mind, a new state of being that is larger than what you were used to and you realize it's because you're not caring unnecessarily about some concern you had. Whether you trick yourself into doing this one afternoon or you work hard for it over time, you're there and lighter. It's wonderful and worth having a diary session about so you can remember what it felt like to be there and more easily get there next time. The goal is for so many 'next times' to happen that this bigger version of yourself becomes your always self.

336. Most schools teach history classes about politicians and war. Few teach art history, artists to look up to, and how they became the artists they became. Thus, many of us need to embrace self-teaching. It takes some discipline and scheduling but the payoff is epiphanies and intellectual flexibility which is crucial for long-term success.

337. **5 components of a healthy relationship with art:** has fun with the process; pride in body of work; realistic goals; treats art as a profession *and* hobby; done consistently with appropriate breaks

338. **Being artistic is one of an artist's good qualities:** so is, being kind [to themselves and others]; curious [about people, eras, and ideas]; approachable [for friends, fans, and strangers]; patient [with listening, feeling, and understanding]; generous [with creativity, time, and destiny]

339. Language can be so colorful when it's right.

340. **Helpful thinking styles when viewing art:** Curiosity→ How was this art made? Emphatic→ What did the artist go through to make it? Imaginative → What could be added? Historical → What came before and after? Student → What am I being taught?

341. Work at things and things will work out.

342. A renaissance is a movement on the move.

343. Free time is me time.

344. **Gifts to get an artist (share with family):** subscription to Ovid (documentary streaming); socks with print of their favorite painter (Haring, Vermeer, etc.); $20 Barnes and Noble gift card; a massage; a planned beach/hike day

345. Art is there to help you identify your feelings.

346. Anybody who takes art too seriously should be stuck in a room and forced to watch cartoons and read joke books until they start predicting the punchlines.

347. At any given time a person has at least a hundred different potential breakthroughs that are just an observation / adjustment away.

348. Books are my cigarettes and I'm a chain smoker.

349. You can discuss my style when I pass away. For now, you can discuss my 'style so far.'

350. Make your art as varied as you are and it will be inherently complex, worthwhile, and fascinating.

351. The most common motivation to make art is fun. You'll use fun every day. It's the most important short-term motivation, and it's also the root of love, which is the most important long-term motivation.

352. **6 ways an artist can mix-up their routine:** wear mismatched socks; eat breakfast for dinner; consume none of the medium you usually do and swap it for a new one; move your bed somewhere else in your room, preferably near a window; put more gel in your hair; drive to a library three towns over and work an afternoon there

353. Run your mouth and see where it goes.

354. To see the light sometimes you have to take a shot in the dark.

355. Speak your filthy mind and that'll clean your conscience.

356. Some artists are wily enough to look at a snake pit and see a ball pit.

357. Ideas are like animals wandering from one person's head to the next, seeing if they'll be welcome. Once they find a home, they have babies and that person finds themself the beastmaster of a wildlife reserve, feeding, playing, training, and ultimately taming that corner of the world. Remember to occasionally leave the gate open. Do it at night and who knows what presents your friends will bring back tomorrow morning.

358. You're never too old to admit that you're young at heart.

359. *"Youth is in the heart and beauty is in the eyes. Life is in the doing and skill is in the tries. These four notions buoy up mankind. See to it that it has a steady supply."* — an invitation to artists.

360. Learning is how you make your big inner spirit big in the first place. Around us is the world of trees and animals and yet there is a place inside you that's bigger. It's big because you make it so. You take a

book off of a shelf and spend an afternoon with it and you end up with that book inside of you. The great people…the leaders… scientists…songwriters… they say so much because of what they've taken in. There are billions of ideas. You carry and develop yours and they are a bit like pets because you love and watch over them and they are also like real children because they have a life of their own eventually, befriending other people and carrying on without us. Ideas are wild things and they make up our spirit.

361. How to make a good racket: take a stance on something that nobody else in class would, like saying birds are the future of transportation or that the principal has a twin she doesn't want us to know about. Take it to the extreme and say it like it's true. At the end somehow show the class how far you've taken it, maybe by bringing up the innocent origin or adding some other twist.

362. This may disturb pessimists: my words are art, your words are art, our conversation is art, food is art, your reflection is art, what you see out the window is art. The most pessimistic pessimist has four or five timeless poems inside him. He has loves.

363. Be friends with everybody. Everybody ultimately is cool in their own way and you get more fun out of things when you are friendly with everyone. You go on more adventures. You have more chances for

random things to happen. Plus you never know when you'll need an accomplice.

364. Make up words and act like they're real. That's how all words came to be, believe it or not. Slang is more real than the dictionary.

365. Make up a universe.

366. Hi, followers, what do you think about going in on a pact to say if any one of us wins the lottery — a big one, more than $1,000,000 — then they split it with the other 4,999? We passed 5,000 followers and it made me think. I'm not saying we should play the lottery because it's low odds but if we do, if someone wins, let's spread it. If I win, I'm down to split. Let me know in the comments if you are. Could be a fun activity.

367. Life happens everyday.

368. Learning is the most interesting thing you could dedicate yourself to. It encompasses everything.

369. I believe in eyelashes, 11:11 and birthday wishes.

370. One of the best art education system in the world is called Dedicolas which is an acronym for Documentaries, Essays, Diaries, Interviews, Collections Of Letters, and Autobiographies. This heap of words mean:

firsthand information. Who would know the most about art and how to make it? The artists. They have the information and experience for us to study. The information for whatever reason has not made its way into a coherent, frequently-taught body of knowledge like mathematics and history and science has but it does exist, can be self-taught, and is called Dedicolas.

371. The process is: obey the rule, internalize the rule, reformulate the rule and go your own way.

372. As staring at a light bulb leaves the bulb's impression on your vision, so too does staring at someone else's work.

373. Contagious writing styles: Bob Marley, Hunter S. Thompson, Sylvia Plath, Ray Bradbury, Bob Dylan, Brian Wilson, David Attenborough, E. B. White, Truman Capote…

374. **11 Point Plan** — Number one. Awaken artists across the world to the idea of artists being unified. Number two. Encourage artists to write their processes and ideas. Number three. Organize ideas into a curriculum. Number four. Implement curriculum into educational system. Number five. Raise children on artistic concepts. Number six. Create art with imagination and empathy. Number seven. Seek jobs that employ creativity. Number eight. Develop an audience for the work.

Number nine. Establish new economic norms. Number ten. Coexist and mature with technology. Number eleven. Repeat until utopia.

375. I want to write a guide to tripping and a guide to anyone who wants to guide someone through tripping. At a certain point these guides will become one because at a certain point a person guides their own trip.

376. I don't really make decisions. I just follow myself wherever I go.

377. **5 reasons to mark up your books when you read:** when you interact with the text, you remember it more; it creates a diary of your experience; when you re-read, you can get right to your favorite parts; pass the book down to someone and they can get a piece of you; it's your book, so, why not?

378. Yearners, learners, students, askers, wonderers, and wanderers; searchers, seekers, seers, flyers, finders, and ponderers; borrowers, builders, creators, and makers; conjoiners, imaginers, chefs, and bakers; instigators, doers, correlators, and connectors; drivers, pilots, explorers, and questers; adventurers, rummagers, lookers, and witnesses; detectives, investors, and risk-takers earn privileges. They earn themselves and the world around them wisdom, knowledge, and epiphany; symphony, mystery, life, and liberty. They earn achievement, fulfillment, happiness, and newness; sky-high, world-wide, mountainside union-ness.

379. **5 reasons to watch movies:** stimulates imagination; teaches empathy; improves critical thinking and narrative comprehension; varies a person's schedule; provides 'small talk' material

380. Lawmaking is an art. So is dentistry, landscaping, and being a museum tour guide.

381. Get some heroes, at least five, e.g., Ruth Bader Ginberg, Studs Terkel, Mr. Rogers, Hayao Miyazaki, Kendrick Lamar. Life is wonderfully complex and you want to see how others navigated and succeeded. Learn their life's story and then life's work.

382. **4 ways of changing for the better:** give yourself opportunities to practice; keep rolling when you're on a roll; create distance from less desirable habits; embrace new methods, ideas, and experiences.

383. When creating: develop a theme; be specific; carry things almost too far; let complexity naturally develop; enjoy the results.

384. When making art: try to act naturally; enjoy yourself; allow for experimentation and try not to critique as you go; interrupt yourself; or use social media.

385. Every artist is a contributor to art history.

386. **Art myth #7,926** Art requires pain, trauma, conflict, seriousness, and inevitable failure. **Art truth #8,377** Art making can be like a kid playing with toys and making up voices and characters effortlessly, dreaming out loud.

387. How to make emotionally arousing content:

     - Create something that can be agreed or disagreed with

     - Be inspired by lusts and disdains

     - Empathize with the intended audience, their current beliefs

     - Voice what's unvoiced; sing their unsung songs

388. **Five ways curiosity is life-changing:** introduces lifestyles of reading and travel; creates habits of asking, talking, and listening; is contagious and attracts like-minds; brings satisfaction when answers are found; keeps a person humble and student-minded.

389. **How to make emotionally arousing content:**

     - Create something that can be agreed or disagreed with

     - Be inspired by lusts and disdains

     - Empathize with the intended audience, their current beliefs

     - Voice what's unvoiced; sing their unsung songs

390. How supply and demand works:

     - Audience demand content

- Creators supply it

- The bigger the audience is, the bigger the demand

Low supply + high demand = throne for the taking

High supply + high demand = competition

Low supply + low demand = not a market (yet)

High supply + low demand = flea market (so far)

391. **5 ways to hear first-hand artist experiences:** interview transcripts; autobiographies; diaries; collections of letters; essay collections; bonus — documentaries

392. Try your best to do your best.

393. Everyone is unique for unique reasons.

394. Art history is our history.

395. Artists are independent together.

396. Art is as close as it is humanly possible for you to get paid to be yourself.

397. Ever wonder what it would be like if an artist was born in a different era, if Edgar Allan Poe was a scriptwriter for the *Twilight Zone*, if Hunter S. Thompson was a political journalist during the Trump era? Oh, the things they could have came up with…

398. Aside from the giving and receiving of love from family and friends, art making is one of the few perpetually healthy activities in our life.

399. Mother Nature is history's greatest content creator.

400. Read this book today and read it again in six months and again in twelve. Each reading will be more vivid than the last. Eventually, you'll be able to share the ideas and talk to others about them as if you'd always known them, as if they had always been yours.

Behind The Eyes

This is my first book. I've written secret books that I've never printed but this is the first one that's gotten into the wild. Thank you. It is a book of one-liners and one paragraph-ers and, somehow or other, they all have to do with art. How cool is that? How cool is it that you bought it? I have a small Instagram and don't know how you found me. I feel like I want to tell you a secret. I want to say something profound and communal as if we're in a tree house together, late at night, swapping plans that we're going to use tomorrow at school during a prank.

stares out window

I've been writing about art since January 14th, 2016 when I left Complex Magazine to write my first book. It's not until I made my Instagram a daily project in the summer of 2019 that I realized how many other artists were in the world. As it turns out, there are many of us and we use our imaginations and would love to use them more. Maybe I can tell you how I wrote these one-liners. That's sort of a secret. The method is to find something in your heart that you feel is true and then say it out loud until you find a way of saying it in the fewest possible words. At first, it might take me a few paragraphs to explain myself. Then I can get to my point and explain it in a paragraph, then a sentence, then a short sentence. Before I know it, I'm able to speak a whole idea in four or five words. "Feel free to feel free." Yeah! I've spoken many times about relaxation and naturalness when it comes to making art. Eventually, "Feel free to feel free" came out. "Feel free…" is me telling you to feel comfortable doing what it is I'm about to ask you to do. Which is? Feel freedom, feel whim. So, "Feel free to feel free." Funny how that one worked out.

Okay. That's what I'll do, explain the back stories. My favorite line of all time is one of my earliest. "If you study enough, one day you will be studied." That summarizes my philosophy — study and you will lead an interesting, accomplished life that other people will be curious about and want to learn from. I would tell myself this when I was writing my first book, sitting in bed, reading and researching. I would sit cross-legged, against the wall, eyes running left to right, occasionally closing the book in my lap, tilting my head back, and thinking. Then I'd open the book and repeat. I read a book every three days for a year. If I could draw, I could illustrate that room from memory because I've spent so much time there, in that same spot. Now it's not the best motivation to want other people to appreciate you. You should work because you yourself enjoy working and find it cool. But looking to the future can put things into perspective. The quote means, "The rewards are later. Think about the appreciative people of the future." I was thinking about myself, actually. I was digging backwards in time by reading old books. Those authors probably didn't realize how helpful they would be to me in the year 2015. I thought, "Let me write for the sake of a future Austin."

Many one-liners come out of the air. I'll be thinking about a concept for a while and begin a sentence like, "If you study enough…" and as I complete the end, the blank naturally fills, "…you will be studied." The beginning is what was on my mind and the ending is my mind synthesizing information. I had thought before about how important it was for me to study and, separately, how grateful I was for old writers. The ideas merged suddenly.

Let me look at the one-liner list and see if there are others like this….

a moment later

"Studying irrelevant art proves there is no such thing." This and the last line are from the *Imagination* chapter of my first book which is my favorite chapter of that book. (The imagination is the coolest thing ever.) I wanted to say, "Studying irrelevant art…" because that is what I was doing at the time, reaching towards old books that few people read. Doing this would teach me great secrets? Be worthwhile? Make me appreciate old stuff? Yes, yes, and yes. They would prove that there was no such thing as irrelevant. Everything is as relevant as I make it. As I said the first three words, the thought itself imploded. "Studying irrelevant art proves there is no such thing."

If you're new to writing and want to learn, look at the writing you read as somebody's real voice speaking the words. In this way, you can train your own mind to think of cool sentences because it thinks of writing as speaking. As long as you talk a lot, cool sentences will come.

"There is a temple between your temples." This was written in the opposite way of the other one-liners. I didn't think, "Hmmm. I want people to regard their mind as a temple. Let me say, 'There is a temple...' Oh! '...between your temples.' That works!" I didn't think that. Instead, I had written a few one-liners and noticed how harmonious sentences sounded when I used the same word two ways so I sat in bed and thought of random words. 'Temple' popped into my head. The line wrote itself. It happened to create a profound truth which makes a reader revere their intelligence and respect themselves more. But that was chance. I could have said, "Bears bear their bearings," which makes no sense. (Still interesting though.)

"A museum is what you get when a genius is a hoarder." This is a banger. It isn't about a fancy grammar or synonym trick. It's pure idea. It uses three strong nouns, "museum," "genius," and "hoarder" which are words that you don't hear often but are familiar. I was looking at my bookshelf and reflecting on the size of the collection. I was also reading the Ray Bradbury essay *Go Not To Graveyards* which is about him being buried in a museum. I said out loud, "A museum is what you get when a genius..." I could have said, "...holds onto a lot of stuff," "becomes a pack rat," "can't say 'no' to free crap," "has to check the bargain bin of every store..." I was aiming for that sort of concept and "becomes a hoarder" was the quick, powerful way of putting it that my brain came up with. It pokes fun at the genius and at the same time is true. If you've ever seen a documentary with an artist who has a huge collection of well-curated and labeled knick knacks, you know what I mean. It's someone who cares for a long time about a certain family of objects.

I wrote these one-liners between January 2015 and October 2019. In that time I wrote five-ish books: *How To Go Viral & Put Wings On Ideas: A Book For Content Creators and Artists*; *100 Questions Every Artist Should Have The Answers To*; *How To Teach Yourself Art When You Know Nothing About It*; *The Word Artist Means A Lot Of Things*; and *Walden 2*. By reading this book, you get the jist of alllll of that. It's like a PlayStation 2 demo discs from a video game magazine from the 1990s. You get a bit of everything. This bonus chapter is an Easter egg.

whistles

"Thinking is fishing your mind's sea." This also is a Top Ten favorite sentence that comes from the *Imagination* chapter of my first book. I was thinking about thinking for ages. When writing *Imagination*, I would ask myself every day, "What is the imagination really? What is happening as I sit here and think? What is going on in my brain?" I would think about how athletics was pushed as far as it was because you could see what an athlete was doing. You could videotape them and if an athlete wanted to throw farther they could adjust their shoulder or push more with their ankle. With the imagination, everything was intangible and invisible so knowing what you were doing was trickier. I've imagined the imagination as a collection of butterflies with each idea being a butterfly and me walking around with an impossibly large butterfly net. Occasionally one butterfly will fly out and sit on my head and that'll be the idea I'm thinking about at the moment. The ideas fly around me, landing and departing. Maybe two or three will sit on my head and that'll be my way of combining ideas. I've also pictured the imagination as a beach with sand castles representing ideas and they get bigger as time goes on. You read about that in my first book. That's the metaphor I settled on. The metaphor I loved but didn't use was the idea of the imagination as an ocean and ideas being fish. Starting in 2013, I would go with my Dad and uncles to Montana to go fly fishing. I spent heaps of time on the Yellowstone lake, waiting, fishing, and I realized that me waiting for fish was like me waiting for ideas. It wouldn't look like I was doing anything if you saw me. But I was. I was looking at the bobber and the way the water moved and if there was any foam or rocks. I was stationary but active. The same goes for thinking. The beauty of this sentence is how brief it is. I introduced a concept with one word, "Thinking…" a sort of mystical and unstudied concept, and five words later I created a visual metaphor. There is an endless ocean with no final border. There are infinite fish down there and all you have to do to catch one is think. The writing lesson here is: come up with metaphors for hard-to-describe things. If you want to come up with a new and original sentence, think about moments where people say, "Oh, it was indescribable," or, "It's so hard to put into words. I'm speechless." Think about those moments and try to put them into words. You'll come up with amazing things.

"Sometimes the most productive thing you can do is stare out the window." So much of art happens in your mind that finding interesting ways to encourage yourself to think, ways to allow yourself to feel free, is helpful. Time and time again, I would look out a window and come up with a solution without expecting it. Then I wrote the one-liner. It has a memorable jolt because it sounds counterintuitive. Sometimes writing or being at the keyboard isn't the best thing. Sometimes it is better to forget what I am doing and solve a problem subconsciously.

"Ride the elephant in the room." This one-liner was made with a new technique. It was inspired by Mark Twain, an old writer from 200 years ago who wrote *Huckleberry Finn* and *Tom Sawyer.* In his autobiography, he had a line, "…the feather that broke the camel's back." The original, more well-known phrase is, "The straw that broke the camel's back" but by changing one word he made the sentence fresh. Let me try that, I thought. I'll challenge myself. I like to exercise my brain muscles just like when I was back in school and a teacher would assign an assignment that I wouldn't choose to do on my own but would ultimately give me a new random skill. I was silently thankful. The challenge here was to be my own teacher and she said, "Find a popular phrase and twist it! Change a concept and you might find something more interesting than what you started with." Okay. Fine. "Elephant in the room." It means there's an awkward subject people aren't talking about but that everyone is aware of and probably should be talking about it. My style as a person and writer is to put that stuff front and center, to make the elephant known so we can properly examine it and see it for what it is. Writing this one-liner was easy because elephants are visually impressive. There are many things to play off of. "I'm going to lead the elephant to water." "The elephant knows the elephant is in the room." "You can smell the elephant in the room." The simplest and most honest sentence was, "Ride the elephant in the room." Add a verb and presto. There's a complete philosophy and visual. This one-liner is a combination of: me being inspired by Mark, me challenging myself, and my personality twisting a tried-and-true truth.

I am the best writer alive. Just kidding. I'm listening to Lil Wayne.

"It is only a matter of time before this moment becomes nostalgic." You are reading this one-liner book and there will be a day, months from now, when you come back to the book and re-read the line and remember the original day. "Oh, that was a great day and I've accomplished a lot since then." It's nostalgic. I like setting up moments for readers like that, aha moments. That's the way I am in real life. I'll tell a joke in a group and see one person's face and know that they understood it and I'll say, "You caught that," and we'll both laugh. Or if I'm with one person I'll say something outrageous with a straight face and for a second they'll have an expression like, "Did you really just say what I think you said?" I'll crack a smile and they'll know I was joking. For that moment, there was surrealness.

"If you are alive, you are young." When thinking about people, I think of us first and foremost as brains. We have pink play-doh in our heads and it's capable of learning and remembering and developing. It so happens that the body around it can only live around 80 years so a lot of what the brain thinks about is contextualized to that life span. If I'm 40 years old and not an astronaut I might think to myself, "Well, I'll never be an astronaut." Or, "I'll never be a piano player" or, "I chose too many forks in the road to go back." But my brain itself is capable of learning everything an astronaut needs to know. If I had the time, I could learn piano. If minds could live for a thousand years, we could learn every talent and language and instrument. In this way, I'm breaking the idea that because someone is old they should consider themselves knowledgeable in their field and unable to become knowledgeable in other fields. Not everybody thinks this but I have seen people hold this belief subconsciously before. Therefore, I remind myself that at any age, I am young. I can pursue each day as ambitiously as if I have every chance in the world to pursue it to its maximum. Biology may not agree but oh well.

"Choose your profession based on which will give you the most orgasms." This one-liner is self-explanatory. It means become a pornstar.

"Studying history helps you realize that it just started." The more I read about artists, the more I saw that historically significant breakthroughs in style had happened only yesterday. I discovered Ernest Hemingway and how he brought simplicity to writing. Writing had been trending since the Victorian and Shakespeare era from flowery, complicated, big-word-heavy writing to plain-spoken, direct writing and I said, "Well, jeez we only just discovered that so there's got to be an infinite amount of topics we have yet to talk about. Hemingway showed us a new Everest and from the peak we can see a thousand other Everests." Similar stuff happened with Marlon Brando and method acting in the 1950s and Keith Haring with painting in the 1980s. In my second book, I wrote an essay called….*huffs*…*puffs*…..*laughs*….excuse me but I just spent five minutes looking through folders on my computer to find a PDF of that book, scrolling through the book for the essay, finding it, and realizing that the title is, "Is History Young?" How coincidental. Anyway, in this essay, I discuss how every field of study is young and has space for you to contribute to. Oh, and politics and civil rights, come on! The right ways to conduct these things are only just being discovered. They still need to go through generations of testing and tweaking. History is young. The more you study history, the more you see that.

"Dumb luck has a plan for you." The thesis of my first book was *relax and have fun and you will make incredible art*. One way of helping you get into this mode is to know that every artist encounters a thousand and one lucky moments throughout their career. I thought about dumb luck and how it helped me many times in the past. At the same time, I was going to church with my Dad a lot because he was between jobs and I figured I should spend time with him and be a good son. The people in church had a million and one funny phrases that they repeated to ground their faith. One was, "God has a plan for you." I replaced "God" with "dumb luck" and the phrases continued to make sense. "Let go and let God," "God works in mysterious ways," etc…

"Life is a love-led lottery." This further pushes my point. Life is luck plus choices you make. Choices you make develop your lifestyle and they are based on the things you love because what you love, you pursue. I could talk forever about this.

At the present moment, there are 400 one-liners and one-paragraphers in my book. (Let's call it a 'booklet' haha.) If I gave each one 300 words of explanation, that would make 120,000 words and — woof. I'm not sure if I can do all that. Here are a bunch of one-liners I wrote this past month. "Life happens live." "Artists are independent together." "It's best to do your best." "Art history is our history." "Good talkers have good ears." "Everyone is unique for unique reasons." These are about a certain period in my life. I have 6,000 followers on Instagram and am thinking more about community, more about people who are interested in art writing. There are millions, I think. We're out here. I don't know how exactly but this idea is affecting me. Anyways….

"Artists are independent together" came from the song that Rudolph and the dentist sing in the Rudolph cartoon from my childhood. He and Rudolph felt like independents but they wanted to be friends too.

"It's best to do your best." At this point, I was on the lookout for any and all double-duty words. Let's invent some sentences now. "Writing the right word is right." "When you reason with reasons reasonably, you become reasonable." "Individual individuals are individuals individually." These are interesting but how can I make them better? Maybe the secret is to find a double-duty word and over the course of a week think about a particular idea, a strong believe, and sooner or later the belief will collide with the word in a deep way.

"Ideas come easily when you are easygoing." They sure do. It so happens that the word "easy" has a weird form where it takes the word "going" with it and becomes an attitude. I've been thinking about how relaxation leads to ideas. Then the word "easy" came to mind and I messed around. "Ease is easy." "Ease is easy enough." "Ideas come easily when you are easygoing." The idea found the words.

"Practice is doing something on purpose right now so you can do it automatically later." This draws attention to the concept of time. Practice happens now and reward comes later. Certain sentences have a snappiness to them, a witty snap, crackle, poppy-ness because they end abruptly. This is one of them. I created the effect by using the same word twice, "something." When it's used a second time instead of using the word itself I use the word "it." This shortens the sentence and causes a reader's brain to fill in the blank. "Practice is doing something on purpose right now so you can do it automatically later." See how I turned "something" into "it?"

"Set aside time to lose track of it." As you read the sentence, you don't realize I'm going to use the word "time" again but I do and I use it as the last word and substitute it with "it." Hence a snappy, instant double-meaning. "Set aside time to lose track of time?" Nah.

"I am a slacker who works everyday." Slackers may work all the time or not at all or in between. What truly makes a slacker is their attitude. They're laid-back and goofy. I like that.

"Life is a parade of circuses." I was falling asleep and sometimes with my eyes closed, I see random images. I was picturing something similar to the PlayStation 3 menu which is called a crossbar. There are icons going left to right and icons going up and down and they cross like a cross. I pictured the up and down being the passage of time and left and rights being different events. As you go up, different events cross your path and each one has its own mini-world within. I realized this was a visualization of life and I wanted to describe it in a sentence. "Life is…"

"…a parade…" was the first thing I thought of because that string of icons going up and down looked like a series of floats. Then I said, "Okay, if it's a parade then the things parading need to be equally outrageous and impossibly big and a circus is kind of like that, a cousin of a parade. It's a celebration and everybody gets together. A parade of circuses. Yeah! That is outrageous and visual. That is a cool way to think of life."

"Fun father's freshness." Finally, alliteration. Lil Wayne said, "Repetition is the father of learning" and I got obsessed with trying to use "father" and "mother" in one-liners. At the same time, I was obsessed with the word "freshness" which I thought was the perfect combination of "cool" and "new." It was the best trait a piece of art could have. Freshness freshness freshness. Father father father. Fun fun fun. Fun is another classic concept I return to often and all three worked out. "Fun fathers freshness." Have fun and you'll do something new and original. I come to that same conclusion time and time again. Different lines of reasoning bring me there. That's how I know it's true.

"Swimming in the ocean is like living in a painting." I was drunk with my sister and her friends on her birthday at the beach. We were in the ocean floating and I looked and noticed that looking at the ocean is totally different than looking at anything else. It is infinite, blue, and swishing. A few years before, I was in the MoMA and stared for a long time at a Monet painting of water and the beach moment reminded me of it. I put two and two together and said, "This is like living in a painting. Here comes a big wave of paint now. Whooooosh." It also reminded me that if I want to come up with original sentences I should do original things. Do new things or things that I don't do often and I'm sure to come up with fresh observations.

"Glass half-full is more accurate." Another deep philosophy. Perhaps one of my most important. I am an optimist and believe that optimism is more useful and productive than pessimism. Duh. Even if you're in a situation where both are objectively, equally true, the optimistic view will tell you more about the situation and therefore give you a better chance of solving the problem. Pessimism will tell you what's not possible and in that way you could go on forever naming other impossibilities without getting to a useful point. I could say the glass is half-empty of orange juice. It's half empty of beer. It's also half empty of plutonium. But saying, "It's half full of water" is the one statement that accurately depicts the reality and can be a jumping off point for more observations.

Harry S. Truman, President of American from 1945 to 1953, wrote a book *"Where The Buck Stops."* The chapter, "What a good president should do," sadly explains at length what a president shouldn't do, what they should avoid. It includes two sentences about what a good president should do and then goes on for ten pages about pitfalls that would prevent them from doing those things. Well, pitfalls are great and all but if a president was doing fine before they read the book then they've received little advice from reading it. By the title, you'd think they would have learned a lot. In the same way, many articles on 'how to write' or 'how to be creative' tell you what not to do. "Don't be self-conscious.

Don't censor yourself. Don't ask for feedback too early." They tell you all these things to avoid and at the end you're left with the thought, "Hmmm I still want some advice on what to do." *What to do* is much more fascinating to read about and frankly requires more imagination to write about. I could tell you all day about ways to bang piano keys that don't make a song. But the freshest teachers are the ones who can tell me the right order to play something beautiful.

"A genius is somebody who knows how to love." This is another top 10 favorite one liner. Genius is a word we use to describe someone really smart, who maybe has been able to do something since they were young or seemingly without trying, just by natural talent. My first idea of a genius is the TV show *Dexter's Lab* where young Dexter can solve crazy math problems. Well, I changed my definition and now consider those people prodigies, which are their own type of person though they can be geniuses too. Geniuses, on the other hand are just people who are super good at stuff, regardless of age. A person can be a genius about plumbing. You become a genius by knowing something really well and you learn to know something really well because you love it. Love causes you to spend a lot of time with it. This is explained more in my essay, "What is a genius?" found in my second book.

"It takes a couple of years to become a beginner. It takes several to become a natural." This reinforces the genius lines. These one-liners are about redefining words. It's only after playing a lot of piano that I finally have enough tools to start making my own songs and in that way I'm finally a beginner. Similarly, after playing for years and amassing complex skills now I can act as if all of these skills have always been with me, as if I was a natural. I like this way of thinking. It's chill. It seems truthful too.

What do all of these one-liners mean? What do they amount to? Well, they're my life's work. I've written five-ish books and their themes are represented here. You could read these one-liners and get a complete outline of me. In that way, they are introductions. Having read them, you can read the books more easily — accessible art ideas. Yeah!

Thank you to everybody who follows on Instagram and bought this. I've been writing alone for years. I've shown friends and family some stuff but not much. Every idea written was a hunch, was what I felt to be true but wasn't sure about and now suddenly people are telling me, "It's true to me too. I feel the same way." I'm getting messages in my DMs like, "You are my favorite Instagram on Instagram," "Please, keep posting. I check everyday." It's amazing. My encouragement had been from myself mostly, from me thinking, "This is worthwhile. Even if no one reads this, it's a feat for the truths to be spoken at all. It's a feat to speak them in simple language. Keep going. Your idols have done it and you love doing it too."

Will you take this booklet and share it? Can art writing become more popular? If the world's artists knew more about imagination, we would be able to create art at a higher level more consistently throughout our lives. I want to live in that world.

The Journey To 5,000

Now here is an idea for a bonus chapter. How can *you* do what I've done? How can you get an Instagram audience and start selling art? I will tell my story and in telling give tips. My journey started with me leaving Complex Magazine. Well, technically, it started at Complex. My job was to write tweets so I had to read articles and condense them into a sentence, one popcorn of information to share. That trained my critical thinking muscle though I didn't realize it then. After some months I thought, "I can write these articles too. I have opinions about Kanye and Eminem." I wrote an article called *10 Hip Hop Songs That Make You A Better Person* because I thought about how many fans in the world loved hip hop and were sick of defending it against accusations of it teaching bad character. It went viral and got eight million hits and sent me a crowdful of Twitter followers. Whoa! Compliments from random internet people, thoughtful comments. That got me going on the idea of being a writer.

I also figured, "Writing is as close as it is humanly possible for me to get paid to be myself." After a few months of posting articles and doing social media, I managed to go on business trips to Miami and San Francisco where I saw Tony Hawk (awesome). He was like ten feet away and I got even more excited about living a cool life.

At the end of every workday, Complex would send an email that listed the most trafficked articles of the day. I would wonder if the writers knew before publishing whether or not they had a popular article on their hands. I googled, "How to go viral book" and thought, "If you're a writer and your writing goes viral, you can charge your company more per article. Going viral therefore is the quickest way to make a career happen." But my search returned NO BOOKS. I was like, "Hold on." At the time, I was reading Richard Feynman's *Surely You're Joking Mr. Feynman* and E. B. White's *Elements of Style* and Stephen King's *On Writing*. I was like, "I can write my own how-to book about how to go viral. If I had a year, I could do that and the book would definitely become popular. It would literally be about how to be popular and there's enough people who want to know that. Everybody in this office should know it. Everybody at BuzzFeed should buy my book. Every kid on YouTube should be interested in this, which is nearly the whole universe." I called my parents and said I wanted to leave my job and asked if it would be okay to move back home. They supported. They said, "Okay. If you feel that strongly, okay."

I told the HR lady at Complex Magazine that I was leaving to write a book and she looked at me and said, "J. K. Rowling was rejected from seven publishers." That was the first thing she said. I still think about that when I need encouragement. I smiled, "I'm shooting for eight."

I feel like I might be going into too much detail? I was supposed to tell you about things related to growing an Instagram but now I am going super moment-by-moment into my life. Maybe this is for the better.

I thought, "I am the most qualified person to write this. There are marketing professionals who could write this book but they're too busy at work. There are academics who could write this book but they're too institution-y. The only person who could write this book today is a young person raised on the internet and that's me."

In Jersey City, I rode out my lease until May 1st and then moved home to South Amboy. For the next year and a half I wrote that book. I wrote every day and fell in love with writing. I discovered the history of writing and writers before me. I learned what it meant to sit and do one thing all day long and care about it and watch it grow week by week. I learned how to read my work as if I was someone else (for objectivity's sake). That was two years of discovery, personal and artistic. I thought, "Is this what kids do in art school? Lucky bastards." After I finished the book, I sent it to acquaintances who I thought could help me and were kind of in the industry but the general answer I received was, "Publishers only want to publish you if you're already a famous author." Back in the day, publishers would read random manuscripts and an editor might say, "Hey, this is good. Let's take a chance on the kid." But that doesn't happen anymore. They care about followers. If I had 100,000 followers and I sent them a manuscript of just commas, I would get a book deal. If I sent them *Romeo and Juliet* but had no followers, they wouldn't read it. I thought, "Okay, fine." My Mom was wonderful enough to say that I could live home another year and try to market the book so while I did that, whatever that meant, I started writing another book.

I had much to say, many important ideas that I had learned over the past two years that didn't fit in the theme of the viral book, so the second book came out fast. It came out twice as fast and twice as big. My goal was to sit once a day and ask myself an interesting question and answer it. However long that took or however brief, I would do that as an exercise. My first book was written in a somewhat painstaking way. I went over every sentence a hundred times. I could show you each sentence and tell you the earlier versions of that sentence and I could even look at a word and tell you all of the other words that had been in its place. I wanted to get away from that process and develop a new one so I answered 100 questions and ended up with *100 Questions Every Artist Should Have The Answers To,* 111 pages, 60,000 words.

Now I was really doing it. My parents were seeing that I was serious and could write full projects. I stopped trying to get published and became obsessed with my own journey as a writer and the things I was learning on a daily basis. I knew that this experience, the hours I was putting into my writing, was the real thing. This is what life was about. I was lucky to have this chance that many people around the world as well as many of my heroes would have killed for. I was 23–24 years old and being given twenty-four hours a day, every day to write all of my thoughts, to practice, to do poetry if I wanted to, to watch documentaries, to crush seasons of shows. I lived in an intellectual playground.

Suddenly leaving Complex for a year or two or three didn't bother me. When I wrote my first book I jokingly said that if it made me $40,000 it'll have been worth it because that was the salary I left. But now I didn't care how much money or years in the industry I missed because it was better to develop writing skills as a young person and apply them throughout my life rather than work as a young person and try to break away and become an author later.

A year passed and I wrote a third book, *How To Teach Yourself Art When You Know Nothing About It*. It regurgitated everything I learned over the past three years, the epiphanies, books read, and documentaries seen. I started writing *Walden 2* and *The Word Artist Means A Lot Of Things* at the same time and while writing these books I decided I would be a writer forever and that this would be how my life would go.

Writing about art became the coolest thing ever and I became passionate about the lack of good art books out there. If you wanted to learn about art and you knew nothing about it other than the fact that you were curious about it, you'd run into three things: academic books which were damn near impossible to be read if you didn't first learn their dense style; old books which were also hard to read but for their own reasons; and books that were kind of what you wanted but not really. For example, you might read a biography about a writer but a lot of the book would have to do with their personal life drama and not so much with their creative process. The creative process is the honey you want to eat but the book is a big romp through the jungle. It's a nice story but it's not quite art writing.

Art writing is…. a term I made up. It means writing about the creative process, about how the imagination works. Now that I had my own personal genre and a backlog of material, I changed directions. After years of keeping my head down, working on my talent, and letting publishing figure itself out, I thought, "Well, now I have to try getting noticed, somehow get popular on the internet." I never wanted to try before because I knew how much work it was. Creating a YouTube channel for example was a full-time job. On top of being the creative guy who makes the content, actually marketing it and trying to grind through those days of having 0 followers was a mission. I didn't want to do that. Every minute I spent doing that I would rather have spent honing my writing. But what the heck. I chose to start an Instagram. YouTube's algorithm was too punishing. Facebook was dead. Twitter seemed deserted too. At least on Instagram I knew there were artists. I made an account and called it @IdeasIHad.

I also got a freelance job in social media, writing another company's tweets because I turned 26 and lost my Mom's medical insurance. Paying for that was one of her *Must Do's* if I was to continue living under her roof.

@IdeasIhad grew initially because I followed as many accounts as I could and I waited for them to follow back. For example I would follow a hundred accounts who just recently followed Humans of New York and maybe ten would follow back. On my feed, I would post all kinds of writing, lines that I thought were bangers and random lines that I was just having fun putting up. I got myself up to 300 followers and started buying promotions from accounts. My first one was from @KidCassidyFilms which is a film facts Instagram and they had 60,000 followers and charged six bucks for a 24-hour story. I said, would you take $50 for 10? He said yes and I saved myself a dollar a promo. During the first promotion, I got 40 followers. 40 for 5 bucks? That's a dollar for 8 followers. I was hooked. That conversion rate was instant evidence to go, go, go. Paying a dollar to get a real person, a creative-minded person, to look at my work and enjoy it enough to say, "I want to keep seeing this in my feed," was incredible. A dollar for eight people, enough to crowd my room, was enthusing beyond description.

The second person I contacted was @AudioFiles and they scammed me. Their price was even better and they said, "When paying through PayPal, click the 'friends and family' option." When paying somebody I could choose to say that they were friends or that they were a business. @Audio said the 'friends and family' option was "safer for him." I didn't know what that meant and didn't think twice about it. After I sent him the $60, I said, "Hey, when are you going to post?" and I never got a response. I messaged him from my personal account which he answered and I said, "Just wanted to make sure you were dodging me." He never responded to that or to my art account ever again. I learned that 'friends and family' meant me, the sender, would have to pay a certain percentage fee for the transaction and that there was no way to refund it.

Meanwhile, if I said I was buying something from a business that transaction fee would have came out of their side of things and there would have been a refund option. Greeeeeat.

I will make the screenshots of this conversation available because the way he treated me, how nice he was, should say a lot about how a scammer can manipulate you.

The third person I bought a promotion from was @HistoryCoolKids. This was a history account with five hundred thousand followers and a style of posting that included long captions so I knew his readers liked reading. For $50 I bought one 24-hour story. He said about 50,000 people would view the story so it was a dollar for a thousand views and I decided that was fair based on me deciding a thousand people was a lot for a dollar. I didn't care what other accounts charged for or what other people got. All I knew was, in my universe, 1,000 was a lot of people.

It turned out I was right and I got about six followers for a dollar again: 300 total. That was the first time I thought, "Oh shit." I would turn on my Instagram and my notifications were flooded. Hearts, hearts, hearts, hearts. Follow, follow, follow, follows. I would put the phone down for an hour and come back to it and followers would jump from 369 to 420. Everything was exploding and it felt amazing. I was visiting my sister who had just moved to NYC and I said, "Hey, look at this." I faced my phone to her and refreshed the page and she saw the jump. Any regular person who has an Instagram has a certain point of reference for what normal activity is and this was well beyond that. It was magic.

I made a spreadsheet and tracked metrics. Initially it was my followers before and after the promotion. Then the promoter's followers and how many people saw the story and how many people clicked the sticker. Then how many followers I got relative to the sticker taps and all of those ratios: follower per dollar, sticker tap per dollar, follower per sticker tap, etc.

In total I had about $1,500. I wasn't in a rush to spend that but if it would secure my eventual profession in this world, I was happy to chuck it off a rooftop.

After that, it was a summer of trying different promotions from different accounts, experimenting with my images, experimenting with their time of posting, etc. Then I was scammed a second time. I bought a promotion from @GorgeousBrains, an account with a lot of followers, maybe a million, for $50. As soon as I bought the promotion I started getting a crazy amount of follows, a flood of people far bigger than what came with @HistoryCoolKids. And they were separated not by 30 seconds or a minute but semi-seconds, literally gaining 300 people in an eye-blink. I looked at the followers and some had missing profile pictures or had only uploaded a few pictures or their bios were not in English and I went to @GorgeousBrains and asked, "Are you sending me bots? Stop, please, if you are." They were like, "Huh?"

Remember what I said earlier about a scammer being too nice to me? It happened again. Before I bought the promo, @GorgeousBrains said, "Before the process of payment, you have to agree that we'll choose the post together. The post should also be the first post in your feed because people that are going to visit your account are most likely to follow it if they see the post that brought them to you." I thanked them for the tip and agreed. I sent them some of my favorite posts as potential promotions and they gave me feedback on which they liked best. It was a nice back-and-forth.

When I confronted them about bots, they sent me screenshots of the statistics on the post so far and asked, "What do you mean?" It looked fine. Afraid to accuse a potentially innocent person, I said, "Okay, I guess I'm not used to being promoted by an account that has such an engaged follower base. If they're all real people then this is a beautiful thing. I've had some dubious things happen to me by promoters in the past so don't take it personally. I want to make sure you didn't make some program send a bunch of fake accounts to me."

They said, "LOL. Now I understand. Listen. We like your account. I personally like your work. We don't play games. That's not funny to even think about. We have lots of readers around the world. All of our clients are fully excited to work with us because we provide the most reliable promotions that actually work."

I said, "Can you send me a screenshot of the sticker taps?" Their first image of statistics was just of views.

They said, "What do you mean?"

I sent them an example.

"We just sent that to you. What do you mean? Oh you mean who clicked on the tag. Okay."

They sent it but this time not as a photo but as a temporary photo and I think I have a screenshot saved somewhere and there was something fishy about it but I can't remember what. They added, "We don't really like the skepticism. We don't usually deal with this. We respect your experience with other pages but if you want to work with us you have to go our way. And trust us. We put 100% effort into our clients. Please consider all the above if you want to work with us in the future."

I said, "I am an inexperienced person in a new environment. Compared to other promotions I've gotten, yours is a hundred times better than theirs. I know bots exist so I wanted to make sure they weren't happening here. I trust you now and believe your followers are real and am therefore overjoyed with my experience. Thanks for taking the time to answer my questions."

They said, "Thanks for understanding" and that was that.

The next day, after I gained 1,500 people in a day, pushing me to 2,400, I decided to buy fake followers. I doubled down and grew to ten thousand this way. Remember when I said that I could send a manuscript of commas to a publisher and if I had ten thousand followers they would publish it? I was right. I broke my piggy bank, bought a hundred thousand followers, and a publisher agreed to publish me the following month. I said, "Are you sure you want to publish a book of just commas?" They said, "We know what we're doing, book boy. We're the ones wearing suits after all." I brushed off the insult, knowing that I had two more hit manuscripts in my drawer at home — one composed entirely of exclamation points and another of semicolons. A year has passed since that day and I am proud to say that you can buy a copy of *Comma, Exclamation, and SemiColon* as a trilogy at a bookstore near you.

Just kidding. I didn't do any of that.

But I did buy followers. I googled how and clicked the first result. The website looked legit enough: $5 for 500 followers. I sent them to a throwaway Instagram account I had. Sure enough, the same flood happened with the same suspicious-looking accounts. I knew then for certain, "I'd been scammed," and this scammer was not going to tell the truth no matter what. They were deep in their lie and had lied the lie a million times before. I asked them for the final statistics and they conveniently said, "Sorry, it's gone." I never responded.

I told this story on my Instagram stories. I told my real followers that I was thankful that they were there and I was happy to hit 2,000 anyway even if many of the numbers were fake. "We're going to keep it pushing because I want that swipe-up feature at 10,000."

Phew. Fast forward more, and now I'm here: a few hundred dollars later, one summer, and dozens of promos. So, how can you do this yourself? The number one advantage I had in this situation was I had $1,500 to start that I could use for promotions and secondly I had four years of material that I could dig through to post to Instagram. By having so much in my backlog, I could post to Instagram effortlessly. If I had started my Instagram and my writing journey at the same time, I might have felt pressure to post even when I hadn't written anything new.

The third advantage I had was that I was a writer, meaning, my product could be created in two seconds. I could write a one-liner and that would be my content for the day. If I was a sculptor, I couldn't sculpt something in two seconds. I could show you another picture of the long-term sculptor I'm working on that I showed you a picture of yesterday but is that that interesting? I don't know. I'm not sure how other artists solve this problem of social media wanting daily content. You can start to involve more of your personal life and show, "Oh, I'm going to the museum today" or "I'm having this nice lunch" but one way or the other you may find yourself wishing you had more content even though that wish has nothing to do with your creative process. It just has to do with the demands of social media, marketing, and blah blah.

If they have the time and they don't absolutely need to become famous overnight, I recommend all artists do what I did which is work on your own time and create relationships with yourself. Working by myself taught me I could do this. I have the discipline. I know how to solve a problem. I know how to come up with a second solution if the first one doesn't work. I'm okay with feedback. I'm okay with having a day's work going unused. I can process these experiences and recognize them as part of my journey.

At this stage, I have a few thousand followers and just announced the creation of this book. About 15 people said that they would be interested in buying it. These are my fifteen favorite people in the world. I appreciate them enjoying my work and supporting me at this baby stage. I'm going to proofread these one-liners and proofread these bonus chapters and that's that.

What does it all mean?

I want to write a third chapter for my book because I feel like it. I want it to be meaningful and for readers to get their money's worth. As cool as 400 one-liners are, we can do better. That chapter may be called, *What Does It All Mean?* Of what importance are these one-liners?

I might as well write the chapter now. The easy answer to my question is that my readers give the one-liners importance. You pay attention to them, consider them, use the ideas and live your life influenced by them and, since the ideas have to do with developing your imagination and empathy, the world becomes a better place. That's a literal answer. That is what happens when someone reads my book, or any book for that matter. Well, the being influenced part. Maybe the better world part depends on the book.

But how do the one-liners come into existence? I write them because I sit and care. My mind has trained itself to look for harmonious words and attach philosophical ideas to them. Presto. Yippee. But I want to go deeper, what do they meeeeean? What does it all mean? They are little pieces of evidence that say, "The world can be better. The world can be more informed, in control of itself, and ambitious." Let me lead by example then. When there are useful ideas, I'll write them and make them easy to get at.

I rarely complain about things because I would rather put that energy towards creating something better that could become popular, and by virtue of it being popular, make the things I don't like less popular. Which I like. If you don't like one political party, put your effort into developing the philosophy and activity of a party you do like. Make it attractive to people. That will create voters which create elected officials and then suddenly your political philosophy is the one in office. If you work in a genre that you feel has some cliches or is too old school for your taste then find a better way, live out that way and your work will find like-minds who will practice your style plus their own and then the version of the genre you enjoy becomes more popular. Then you're happy. Leading by example is one of the most powerful concepts I've come across.

So then, these one-liners mean that I'm living by example, my example. I am showing the world how I would like the world to think. I'm showing it my style, my way of being excited about life.

As much as I love the world, I think it is at less than .1% of its 'excitement' potential. People who are creative have to go to work rather than practice. How many people are born in situations where they are not encouraged or where resources are unavailable? Just being born on the east coast of the United States in a middle-class family puts me in the top 1% of all people, of all opportunities.

I'm getting more messages on Instagram saying, "I have never felt a community of artists around me until I found your Instagram." I've never felt lonely and yet messages like this makes me realize I might be. I am fulfilled in that I have friends who I hang out with and have common interests with but my artistic side has not ever been directly encouraged. No one has ever said, "Practice writing. It's fun." No one has ever said, "Try to learn an instrument. It's tricky but once you get the hang of it, it's worth it."

With my Instagram, I can say those things to people and they can hear it. They can live in a world where art is important. A community appears and asks, "How are you doing? How has your work been going? When can we see your next show?" This feeling, in my experience as someone in the top 1% where there's all of these opportunities and resources, has never been felt. I've never seen it around. How does that make sense? How can I be rich and poor? The answer is, art is not popular. Everybody loves music and movies but the world I imagine is a world where all eight billion people are multidisciplinary artists. We all have huge book collections, love to create, sing, dance, and go out on Friday. We all have friends who we can be expressive with. We have full calendars because of the things we want to experience. And we have artistic opportunities because we don't have to work. We put up a billion windmills on the top of Mount Fuji and have all the renewable energy we need so we can spend our time as we wish. That is the world I want to see and that is the world I'm trying to get to by walking there myself.

The ultimate trick, the most radical trick a person can perform in society is being paid to do what they love. If you can discover how to do that, within the frame of economics that exists in your area (or if you can explode that frame, by all means…), you are a wonderful person who deserves everything they have. Congratulations. I often reflect on how lucky I am to have writing as my favorite art because I can do it from anywhere. I use inexpensive equipment that I always have with me, my brain and mouth, and I think of this in contrast with filmmakers that need a director, actors, and a greater variety of resources. How do you become a professional filmmaker? You have to have one of the few movie studios believe in you and invest millions of dollars and that's a far trickier road, from my limited point of view, than being a writer who can be behind their keyboard all day and conquer the world that way. This is to say, I'm not sure how everybody can lead by example. You all out there reading need to tell me. You need to answer the question yourself, by getting your hands dirty and feet wet. Then tell me how because I am curious. =)

Apparently, I have to live life sequentially. I can't go into the future and realize the right decisions and come back and perform them. I have to learn as I go and make the best of what I have. That can be tricky. I'm lucky in that I'm in my late 20s and maybe, possibly, fingers-crossed, have the ability to make a living based on my writing. That alone puts me in the super 1% of 1% of 1% of 1%. It is so rare for that to happen and yet even though I've used a lot of luck and good fortune in my life, I have also earned this. I've been behind the keyboard every day for four years. I have worked. I would love if everybody else had the opportunity to do what I did, spend a large stretch of time learning their skill and how to make it work in the economy.

That's what these one-liners mean. They mean: educate yourself, become intellectually and artistically capable, and perform that trick. Learn how to make a living doing what you love. You will improve the world.

PS

Each of us represents a fraction of what the world means, what the definition of the world is. By changing yourself, you change the definition of the world slightly. Or more than slightly. A lot can fit in a small space. Infinity can sit on the back of your fingernail.

How To Maintain Your Motivation For A Lifetime

I had finished this booklet with three bonus chapters and that was enough but wouldn't ya know it, I had a fourth quarter itch and dashed off another essay in the parking lot behind a pet food store. This one, I realize, is for super dogs, the super readers who want to see into a master plan of artistic philosophy. This goes beyond one-liners and well wishes. It gets heavy. We go full art-student mode. Okay? We answer a big daddy question in art history, how do you keep motivation for a lifetime? Okie-dokie…

Step 1. Insert yourself into art history.

This means learning about those who came before you so you can see yourself as one of them, capable of living out your own 80-year adventure. In having this transformational experience which may take a year or two or four, you'll discover what it's like to go from a newborn artist to member-of-the-family artist. You'll realize that being an artist is a real thing, that there were people before you who did it and that you are presently participating.

To achieve this broad, psychological goal, read heaps of autobiographies and oral histories and watch documentaries. The adventure of inserting yourself into history is the entire purpose of the third book I wrote which is called *How To Teach Yourself Art When You Know Nothing About It*. It recommends the exact documentaries and books for you to enjoy. More importantly than grouping them into a sensible curriculum, it gives you an idea of what it feels like to read and watch them, the feeling of being piqued. You already know it's the right thing, oh, it's the right homework, but more than that it enthuses you to go on the long learning journey. Life becomes, in a visceral and real way, an adventure. You want to live your own. You realize how much a person can accomplish and how realistic it is. When you work at it, it happens. Art success happens.

It took me years to go on this journey but if you're doing it in your part-time it may take more. Either way, it's a good time throughout. Every documentary will have you amazed. Every book will have you wowing. You will experience ten thousand epiphanies. I would experience ten a night, discovering, "Oh, Amy Winehouse was a songwriter before she was a singer." "Oh, Keith Haring left art school a year early because teachers told him he had learned enough and was better off working on his art full-time." "Oh, Hayao Miyazaki created all of his movies for children." "Oh, John Belushi was warned about going to Saturday Night Live before spending enough years at Second City to learn the fundamentals of improv." "Oh, Hunter S. Thompson typed *The Great Gatsby* over and over to learn F. Scott Fitzgerald's style." There are an infinite amount of moments to interest young artists. Consider this journey mandatory and yet this mandatory-ness is only in the background. On a night-to-night basis, as you encounter and live it, it's fun and it is what student life is. Every artist should experience this. It is the initiation. Once through, you will have a sound, calm understanding of your own place in the art world and history and you will be confident to experiment and go about your business. Which brings me to my next point…

Step 2. Be curious about your business.

Put another way, create your next piece of art because you want to see what you come up with. Be interested in seeing skills you learned during your last project be displayed again. Be interested in stumbling into new skills. Sheer curiosity about your body of work will carry you for a lifetime. Be your own biggest fan, the person who laughs hardest at your own inside jokes and wonders the longest at your own proposed questions.

Make art that you wish you saw more of in the world, experiment with topics that you wish were more talked about. Sometimes I'll want to read something and I'll look at my bookshelf, thinking, "No, not that book…not quite…almost but…" And then I'll realize the book that comes closest to my appetite is my own work. I don't want to read my own books because I already know what's in them so the only way to satisfy my appetite is by writing new stuff to read tomorrow.

Once you are well inserted into your own curated version of art history, curiosity about your own business becomes the ongoing motivation. It's the reason I know I'll be busy for the rest of my life. I love what this artist, Austin Kaiser, comes up with and I'm always going to wonder what's next for him, wonder what else he has to say given that he's already said so much.

Step 3. Answer these questions: do you want to make a living with your art or will it be a part-time hobby? If you want to make a living, how?

Making a serious effort towards transitioning from working your job to making a living with your art, or being okay with working your job for the foreseeable future and making art as well as you can in your spare time are both valid lifestyles. Depending on what your job is and the meaningfulness you derive from it, it might make perfect sense to keep your art on the side. On the other hand, you might feel deeply that you were put on Earth to make art and that doing anything other than making a full-time effort towards it would be depriving yourself of justice.

If you determine that you want to go full-time, the next thing to determine is, what is realistic? I say, regardless of hometown, if you have internet you can become a famous musician, illustrator, and writer. The internet thrives on this stuff and you can go viral. Sculpture, ballet, free diving — these might need an in-person community's support.

When I decided to become a writer I decided based on the fact that writers exist. Whether it's J. K. Rowling writing her own stories or a journalist working for a magazine, these are both known jobs that you can make a career from. I knew that there would be room in the industry for me if I became competent enough to deserve it. On top of that, I had some inherent competency. I'd always been a big mouth and though I hadn't practiced writing specifically, I figured with a year of studying I could learn it well enough to be paid.

How have those before me succeeded, I wondered. Not necessarily the giants from art history but the literal people in my city today, how did they get their start? Are there institutions, communities, resource caves? Where can a young, hungry artist burrow themselves so as to be surrounded by ideas and chatter? Where can one go for sustenance, intelligence, guidance, and maybe contact information for chief editor of the local art kid mag? I must know. Are there secret bars, libraries, saloons, and computer labs where genius congregates and spreads itself to all who enter? Maybe the counselor of my community college would know...

Answering these questions requires pavement pounding and the pounding should be a pleasure. Feel empowered when you find information. Even if the information makes the market seem smaller than you realized or that there are less opportunities, feel empowered because you know that. When you know the truth you can work with it. You can decide not to pursue a career because you know it's truly that difficult or you can forge ahead knowing an adventure awaits. Either way, you are making deliberate decisions in life and that creates meaningfulness which is the ever-present, cake-layer beneath motivation which is itself the ever-present, cake-layer beneath one's outward personality and daily acts.

Tips and tricks

If you are demotivated, and you've done the first three steps, then, to revive your motivation, do one of the steps again. I told you that I spent two years reading all these oral histories and watching documentaries which gave me the presence of mind to know that I was among these people and off on my own journey. Well, while I'm off on my own journey for another bunch of years, I'm bound to have a hiccup or two. I'll benefit from re-watching a documentary. I'll remember what it was like to be that young kid realizing the information for the first time and what it felt like to be juvinated and that in turn rejuvenates my present journey and reminds me that these ups and downs can happen and it's my job to inspire myself. How many times have you listened to your favorite song? Part of the reason you have such a history with it and such feelings for it is because you probably listened to it hundred times. In the same way, that deep relationship is waiting for you with every book and movie. It's a matter of re-indulgence.

I like to read the letters of Hunter S. Thompson because they create a history of his body of work. I see Hunter writing his first book as a 20-year-old, figuring out his style. I see him as a 30-year-old running for Sheriff of Aspen, Colorado, figuring out what his next book will be. I hear him think through his problems and in this way I immediately feel comfortable thinking through my own. I feel like my problems, no matter how vague or profound or seemingly difficult to solve, are just simple human problems. They're things that people of the past have solved and it's now my turn to spend the time. The idea is that art is a straightforward human activity, it's something everybody does and is capable of.

As for the tips and tricks, these are ones you've heard before: change up your routine…go for a run…call up an old friend…go into the attic and find pajamas you wore when you were six-years-old and wear those…press your cheek against the TV and watch it that way…get an inflatable mattress and put it on the nearest river and go your ways…confess a fictional heinous crime to a priest…watch the six-year-olds fall down at the skatepark…anyway you can, rile yourself, poke your brain. Stub your own big toe if you have to.

I'm going to tell you more experiences with my favorite artists and why I love them. That'll give you a blueprint.

E. B. White was the first writer I was introduced to as a post-college big boy. He was a master of clarity and simplicity in that he picked out little pieces of beauty about people's behavior and made me see them. An author has the power to do that and life is so enormous that it takes a billion authors just to see a patch of it. E. B.'s specialty was the farm and city, two environments I love. He spent half of his life on each, a farm in Maine and an apartment in New York City. I immediately connected and saw him as a writing teacher.

He's famous for his essays and each is like a compact movies. They are only a few pages and about a serious event and that made them easy homework for me. I didn't feel like reading a full book so to pop in and see a masterpiece quickly was useful and it was easier for me to practice with.

And he's the first writer I shared with my Dad to get him interested in reading again or, really, for the first time. He connected for the same reasons I did. E. B. was accessible and human and right there.

Studs Terkel is an oral historian and he's got a book, *Hard Times,* where he interviewed people who lived through The Depression and I read it and I was like, "Wow, this moment in time is really real for me. This book is not a book. It's people talking." That got me hooked on oral history. He has another book called *Working* where he interviewed a doctor, parking attendant, lifeguard — basically every profession. It's like getting behind 7-Eleven and talking to the cashier while they're on their smoke break. Between E. B. telling me about the farm and Studs about the world, they showed me how massively powerful plainspoken human voices are. Simple and straightforward feelings and anecdotes have the power of sincerity. I saw universes in those books. Anything could be accomplished writing-wise after I'd seen that.

Thank you, Ernest Hemingway, who I would later learn is famous for his plain-spoken, simple style too. He won a Pulitzer Prize for *The Old Man And The Sea* and that book is only 27,000 words. The first Harry Potter book is a 77,000. A funny side story is that I'm always trying to make my writing simple so I put it into a piece of software that tells me what grade level I'm writing at, like, college level or 12th or 11th grade. I'm always trying to get younger, to make my work as accessible as possible. Over the years I've been able to write consistently at a 9th grade level and that's a huge accomplishment and has taken me a long time to get to and most writers, if I put them into the software, would be at a 12th grade or college level so I was already feeling good but I put *The Old Man And The Sea* in there and it was an 8th grade level. That is the only book I've seen reach that. It's so plain-spoken that if you read the first paragraph, you get sucked in. I don't know how I skipped that assigned book in high school — well, actually I do. I didn't read any books there — but, anyways, *The Sea* could grab anybody who gave it a chance.

And Ernest has a book called *On Writing* and E. B. has one called *Elements Of Style* so these two writers not only wrote in a plain style but they happened to write books on writing. They told us how they do what they do. This is a miracle in the art world, where accomplished artists describe how to be them, how to create in their style, and what their take on art is. It's a rare thing and it helps that these guys were such great writers that they were able to make their own creative processes understandable. Some artists write about their processes but the writing doesn't make sense and it might as well have been written in wingdings.

Then comes Ray Bradbury and I've talked about my love for him so much in my other books that I'm not sure if I'm going to do it here. But he taught me enthusiasm, that's the best way to put it, and I reread his work more than any other writer. Unlike the first gaggle of writers, he isn't plain-spoken. He's lyrical and poetic and visceral and that was a new thing for me to embrace. I saw how I could still apply the rules of clarity and simplicity that Ernest and E. B. recommended while being fantastical and wild. That was a new level of application, a breakthrough.

After that, my influences branched and we can — boy... Stella Adler, yeah, she's an acting teacher and heavy on taking work seriously and looking at it as a craft, something you work on repeatedly. That's a cool attitude to instill.

Hayao Miyazaki directed *Spirited Away*. He has two books of interviews and essays.

Then there was Oscar Wilde and Mike Monteiro and Susan Sontag's diary and *The Bell Jar* and...

....

...

...

What else can I say? The story rolls on. Feeling a part of this great art party, this global, time-crossing, talent-gelling effort to M-A-K-E T-H-I-N-G-S was my, and is your, first permanent entry into the game. Vinyls on my wall and books on my bookshelf represent the other players, history's roster, and, as I like to call them in my essays, our 'deceased cheerleaders.' Stock your own shelf. Staff a cheer squad. This companionship is a forever feeling. The masses of human superheroes, dirty-footed athletes, hard-working problem-solvers, and far-thrusting territory-hoppers make up the Beautiful Life Orchestra, the harmonious experience of Being Here. We adopt them for our benefit. We revere them for our perspective. To cloak ourselves in their achievements is to put on a coat with so many layers and colors that every sort of stray weather debris is buffed and every nourishing ray of sun and cool oath of wind is let to pass. Gosh darn, the weather and crowds are nice. Don't you think? Isn't this a good time to be here? Let's grab a seat. They're starting the next song. Oh, yes, Joan Baez singing *House of The Rising Sun*. Amazing that we should end this book while listening to a song with no known author, a passed down song that many have sung and made their own. Kind of like life, eh? That's a good metaphor.

How To Go Viral & Put Wings On Ideas

A Book For Artists & Content Creators

By Austin Kaiser

You want to make a living creating content but you do not have enough fans. So you go viral. To go viral you need to create a piece of content full of emotion. Then find an influencer to aim their spotlight at the content.

That's the whole process.

The tricky part is making an emotional, viral-worthy piece of content. That's why we will learn about supply and demand, cost and benefit, Andy Warhol, The Beatles, and Mona Lisa.

We'll answer the following questions:

Why do so many trends come from the youth?

Why are memes everywhere?

Why do movie studios release so many sequels?

Why is Einstein famous?

Why is God famous?

How do you look for a vacuum, for white space?

How do you create content in a saturated market?

How do you invent demand out of thin air?

Altogether, this book is a guide to making art and making a living making art.

Contents

Preamble

Become charged with the viral spirit. The formula. The architecture. That you will. But you must also be charged with the spirit of a poet, a humanist, your fan's biggest fan. Their link to fantasy. Scoop a chunk of their brain matter and arrange it into an irresistible pattern of "!!!" and "???"s. To spark virality we must be truly original. We must make contact with a solar flare of thought and momentum. Our viewers depend on us for inspiration and warmth. We can supply it in avalanche, in world-roaring fashion. This is our responsibility. This is our challenge. We are entrusted with the keys to attention. The keys to awareness. Permission to lodge in the brain of millions, rent-free. This is an opportunity. Your ideas and mine should meet, I think. They would be great friends. But that only happens when we make it so. We have the keys to a great wave. An ocean of attention which we can summon and tsunami. We can, for a moment, freeze and thaw millions. Roar a singular call. Invite and be responded to, a global RSVP. We can architect moments. We can stir emotions. Volcanoes. Burst upon, flow over, wave a wand and steal the eyes of millions. We have this power. What can you do with it? What do you have that is worthy? The organic, the serendipitous is beautiful in its own way. But what of the deliberate? The artfully crafted? Hours poured. Spark like a brush fire. You don't have time to waste, and neither does your audience. Explode like a paintball. Remember this music.

By reading this book you will be able to understand everything you see shared on the internet and why it's being shared.

The internet is not full. It is not saturated. Do not be scared by the crowd. There is always room for the exceptional. Your idea. Your spark. You do not need to fight for my attention. Just earn it. Earning attention is easier than fighting for it, or tricking me into giving it to you. And ultimately, more fun. I will teach you how. We are all great consumers. We all are gifted with pink goo that processes, questions, and comes with an unlimited supply of curiosity. I have yet to meet someone who has filled their brain. There is no such thing. And it is for this reason that your idea can win. A new phenomenon, equal parts awe-harnessing and internet-fueled. This thinking is not new. It has been discussed since the dawn of discussion. But now we have something new to talk about. Something new to talk with.

Creating Moments

A moment goes like this: the listener presses play. They hear your song. While they hear the song, miniature hands reach through their headphones and into their brain. The brain extends its own miniature hands which reach and clasp the song's hands. The two become one. Whatever the song does, the listener feels. If the song gets high, the listener gets high. If the song moves, the listener gets moved. After the instrumental plays out and the song ends, the listener turns to their friend, hands over the headphones, and says in the same tone that Bob Dylan used when passing Paul McCartney his first adult cigarette, "Listen to this."

You are probably familiar with these types of vivid moments. They are everyday experiences for people who listen to good music. Or watch good movies.

Martin Scorsese carried me through a moment. I was watching *Goodfellas* when Joe Pesci asked, "Funny how?" Immediately the room got tense. It felt like fishing lines had tied me to my chair. Joe asked again, "Funny how? How am I funny? Am I funny like a clown? Do I amuse you?" The fishing lines got tighter.

Finally Ray Liotta wised up and realized that Joe was joking in his signature psychotic way. Ray said, "Get the fuck outta here." Everyone laughed and the fishing lines disappeared. The tension evaporated as quickly as it materialized. If you had consulted a stopwatch, it would tell you that four minutes had gone by. To us, it felt like one solid moment.

The Beatles carried me through a moment recently too. At the end of the moment I was left with a feeling. It's true. Whether it's the soldier running back into battle to save his friend, the family members who take 12-hour shifts to stay bedside by their sick grandmother, or the painter who spends two years on his back staring at the ceiling he is painting - the soldier, the family, and the painter are motivated by love. All you need is love.

Joe Pesci and John Lennon were the subjects of conversation that night at dinner. My roommates sat around the living room and I played the music, played the movie. One friend said, "I never really got into the Beatles." I said, "You're mad." He went and listened to The Beatles for a week. Another friend said, "We should have a Scorsese marathon." We had one for a week. For seven days, our house filled with the sounds of guns and guitars.

Why tell this story? I tell it because the story puts a magnifying glass on Step 2 of the viral process.

Step 1

Content creator puts emotion into content

Step 2

Someone sees the content and feels the emotion

Step 3

People talk about the content

Step 2 is the 'moment' I have been talking about. To be specific, the moment is a transition. It is the transition from unemotional to emotional, from untalkative to talkative. I was hanging out, minding my business, and then, because art walked in the room, my neck got chills. I went from sleepy to jolted, from hum-drum to bang-on-the-drum.

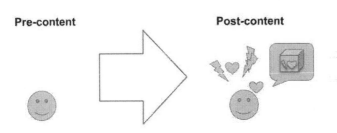

That's the transition.

That transition is our goal. We want people to get an emotion out of our work and bring that emotion to a friend. If we can make a person do that, we can go viral.

To be more scientific, the transition is what biologists call emotional arousal. It's what happens when a person gets riled up. They get sweaty and their heart rate increases and, most importantly, they talk. They become chatterboxes. You can test this yourself by going to a basketball game or riding a rollercoaster. Your mouth with open and stay open until you calm down.

Mystery solved.

You cause emotional arousal. People talk about your content. You go viral.

What's missing?

Step 1.

Put emotion into content. That's a fun part.

Step 2 and 3 accomplish themselves when you do Step 1 really well.

The easiest way to accomplish Step 1 is to take what you hate and destroy it in art. Or take what you love and give it a French kiss. If something is bothering you, stick it on canvas with TNT and blow it away. If there's something that makes you dance, put that on canvas and tango. Loves and hates are the most persistent sources of inspiration in the history of art.

Imagine emotions on a scale from 1 to 10. If you can create happiness at a [6] then 100 people will talk. If you can make happiness at a [9] then 1,000 will talk. Each notch higher gains an exponential amount of conversations. The basic math is, anything under a [5] doesn't get talked about. It stirs no response. 90% of the conversations on the internet are of the few pieces of content that take us to [9] or [10].

Content creators who want to go viral are interested in pushing to [10] at least. We aim for orgasms. We want to be as moving as full moons. For that full moon moment, our audience becomes the canvas. We paint emotions on them.

Below is a list of emotions to get you started.

Nostalgia: a pleasant yearning for the people, places, and life experiences of the past.

Nostalgic content can bring pets, musicians, and old friends back to life. To make nostalgic content, get your photo album, sit next to a window, and remember.

Astonishment: utter surprise and wonder.

We feel astonished when an underdog wins. We expect one thing and get something else. To make astonishing content, add a twist.

Catharsis: letting go of negative feelings associated with old emotions, worries, and events.

Sometimes we bottle up embarrassing or traumatic feelings. Cathartic content allows us to Sometimes we bottle up embarrassing or traumatic feelings. Cathartic content allows us to release them. To make cathartic content, open up to the audience. Let them see a part of you that you hide from yourself.

Outrage: anger that comes from seeing or experiencing injustice.

Outrage is when you scream at a bad situation. You scream in order to express your frustration and warn other people. To make someone outraged, tell them why the situation is bad and why it ought to change.

Enlightenment: when curiosity is satisfied. Being in possession of impressive knowledge.

Enlightenment is when you learn a lesson and feel a shock from the usefulness and simplicity of the lesson. To make enlightening content, come up with a great idea and share it.

Empowerment: feverish optimism about one's capacity for future achievement.

Empowering content is hope in the form of art. It encourages us to shrink the difference between our current self and ideal self, and to celebrate that journey.

You can pre-decide what emotion you want to conjure. I do sometimes. But you can also be yourself, do what you like, and see how that goes. You can think long and intensely about the subtleties of emotion. Or you can let your spontaneity lead the way. You'll probably end up doing both.

Once you are able to take your hands off the wheel and let the information in this book work in the back of your mind, making content can feel like a life goal, like a service, like a combination of game, profession, responsibility, joy, and opportunity. All things are possible through art.

In conclusion.

Going viral is easy. Lots of people have done it. To practice sharpening your viral wits, go to the *Humans Of New York* Facebook page. Each photo is viral and taps into manys emotions. Read the comments and you'll feel plenty. This can be your Square 1 of learning viral design. You can go there for infinite inspiration.

RELEASE DATE: ??/??/2020

Made in the USA
Columbia, SC
20 December 2019